Text copyright © 1972 by Julian May Dikty. Illustrations copyright © 1972 by Bill Barss. International copyrights reserved in all countries. No part of this book may be reproduced in any form, except for reviews, without permission in writing from the publisher. Printed in the United States.

ISBN: 87191-214-7
Library of Congress Catalog Card Number: 72-85043

Sea Otter

JULIAN MAY

Illustrated by Bill Barss

Creative Educational Society, Inc., Mankato, Minnesota 56001

She was born in the ocean, off the shore of California. She looked like a wet, furry toy with shiny black eyes. Her mother licked her carefully after birth, then laid her on top of floating strands of seaweed. The baby sea otter bobbed peacefully in the water. She could not swim, but her thick fur coat held her up like a life jacket.

Other sea otters floated all around the mother and her pup. Many were on their backs, with their feet stuck up in the air. Others rested lower in the water, their large hind feet moving slowly like flippers to keep them from drifting away. The sun shone warmly. A few white gulls flew overhead.

The mother otter was tired after giving birth. She slept beside her pup. After awhile the baby was hungry. She gave a soft, mewing cry. The mother took the baby onto her belly and hugged it. The she-pup drank rich warm milk from two nipples hidden in the mother's fur. Then she slept again, wrapped in seaweed, while her mother dived for food.

Down, down, the mother otter went. Her body moved swiftly, like a furry torpedo. The webbed hind feet drove her toward the sea bottom, 40 feet down. She searched until she found an abalone, a large sea-snail. It was fastened to the rock. The otter kicked it and pulled at it. It stuck tight. She picked up a stone and smashed at the shell until the abalone came loose. Then she carried both snail and stone to the surface.

There she floated on her back, the stone resting on her belly. She grasped the abalone in both forepaws and raised it back over her head. *Clink! Clink!* With all the power of both front legs, she smashed the tough abalone against the rock again and again to break it open. Then she ate the delicious meat inside.

Of all living things in the world, only a few besides man can use a tool. The chimp will use a stick to get food. A small bird from the Galapagos Islands uses a thorn to pick insects out of twigs. The Egyptian vulture breaks the strong eggshells of ostriches by dropping rocks on them. The only other tool-using creature that we know of is the sea otter, with its anvil stones.

When the mother otter finished her meal, she rolled over and over to wash her soiled fur. She combed it with her claws and groomed it with her teeth. Only if it was clean would it be dry and waterproof. This fur was the softest, thickest, richest fur of any animal. It kept the otter warm in the coldest sea water—but only when clean.

The otters spent the afternoon resting and drifting and resting again. The mothers kept their babies with them. Small pups rode their mothers' bellies. Larger babies floated beside their mothers, heads and paws sprawled across the mothers' bodies. The male otters stayed away from the mothers with babies. They were larger than the females, up to five feet long and weighing as much as 80 pounds.

One large male was the leader of the herd. As the sun dropped low, he gave a soft signal cry. At once, the entire herd of 50 otters dived with a splash. The mothers clasped their babies to their chests. Coming up again, the otters began swimming toward their favorite feeding place about three miles away.

They were only two miles offshore. Farther out in the ocean, three black-and-white killer whales leaped from the water. They were warm-blooded sea dwellers like the otters, intelligent hunters that sometimes chased and caught members of the herd. The otters stopped swimming. Several rose up in the water, shaded their eyes with their paws, and kept a wary watch until the killer whales were out of sight.

Once their enemies had disappeared, the otters began to feed. They dove into waving "forests" of giant kelp, as tall as trees. They brought up many sea urchins, crabs, abalones, and clams. Some caught fish. The otters could not remain under water, as fish could. They had to come up for air at least every four minutes.

From everywhere came the sounds of otters breaking shellfish on rocks. The old leader did not dive for his own food. He waited until another otter cracked open a morsel—then stole it. No otter objected. He was the king of the herd and could do as he pleased.

When every stomach was full, the herd traveled to its favorite sleeping place. The otters cleaned themselves like cats. Some itched from the bites of flea-like parasites. They scratched and splashed until they felt better. Then they all wrapped themselves with ribbons of kelp to keep from floating away. And as the moon came up over the California shore, the otters slept.

The she-pup fed only on her mother's milk for the first months of life. Later, she began to eat sea animals that her mother brought. By the time she was a year old, she no longer needed milk. The mother cared for her little one with great devotion. When winter storms came, she held the baby tightly so that she would not be washed away.

The pup slowly learned to swim and dive. She played with the other young ones in the tall surf and hid among underwater rocks. Sometimes, the otters went on land. They walked in a comical, humping way because of their short forelegs and large, webbed hind feet. But once they returned to the water, they were graceful and beautiful.

Besides the killer whales, the only natural enemies of the otters were sharks. Sometimes, when otters fought over a mate, blood would flow into the water. Sharks could smell it for long distances and might seize the wounded otter. But such attacks were rare. Most of the time, the herd was left in peace.

The herd lived near the southern end of a State Sea Otter Refuge, a part of the coast set aside by law where human fishermen were not allowed to go. But sea otters cannot understand human laws. Sometimes the otters strayed outside the refuge, near the fishermen's boats.

These men hunted abalone. They dived down and gathered the giant snails and sold them at a high price as a luxury food. Sometimes, otters and divers met in the abalone beds. And then there was trouble.

The fishermen knew that the otters ate many abalone. They also knew that, for some reason, it was getting harder and harder to find the prized shellfish. So when they saw otters, the fishermen clubbed them and chased them— even though this was against the law.

Some men even hid on the cliffs above the otters' resting grounds and shot the animals as they drifted peacefully in the sea.

All through man's history, he has taken animals for his own profit. Thinking only of his needs for the moment, man has hunted some mammals, birds, and sea creatures until they all but disappeared. The great herds of buffalo vanished. The fur seals nearly disappeared. Even the sea otters were hunted for their fur until they almost vanished from the earth.

Sea otters were saved, just in time, by laws that protected them from fur hunters. And so their numbers slowly increased. They filled the otter refuge and tried to spread into the places where otters had lived long ago—before the time of the fur hunters. As the young female otter grew older, she herself strayed from the refuge into the fishing grounds.

At first, the fishermen did not notice her. She swam with a small herd of young otters. Whenever they heard the sound of a boat, they fled.

In many places outside the refuge, the giant kelp forests were disappearing. Sea urchins, which ate kelp, cut through the stalk of the giant seaweed and allowed it to drift onshore. The young sea otters ate many, many sea urchins—just as they did inside the refuge. But there were only a few otters, so the numbers of sea urchins became larger and larger.

As the kelp vanished, so did the abalone, which lived in the kelp beds. Strangely, as the fishermen destroyed the otters, they were also helping to destroy the abalones that they wanted to save.

One day, a boat came into the bay where the otters liked to rest. The animals became very frightened when the men came after them. But these men had no guns. They were wildlife experts, and they caught the young female otter and her companions in nets and hauled them into the boat.

She was shut up in a dark box. The box moved. There were strange, frightening sounds—but she did not know that she was taking an airplane ride. She only crouched, silent and afraid, and waited for the box to open again.

She saw daylight and fell through the air. *Splash!* She was in the sea again—but in a part of the sea she had never seen before. The wildlife men had taken her and her companions more than 100 miles away, to a new place where the otters would be safe from man's dangers. Next year, she would take a mate and have a pup of her own. And a new colony of sea otters would begin to grow along the California shore.

ABOUT SEA OTTERS

The sea otter is a member of the weasel family, closely related to the river otter. Adults are from four to five feet long, including the foot-long tail. The fur is brown, blackish, blond, or a mixture of these colors. The forelegs are short, with small, clawed feet, while the hind legs are longer with large, webbed feet. The animals have keen hearing and eyesight. Their teeth and jaws are powerful, enabling them to crush shellfish easily.

When man does not frighten them, sea otters are friendly and curious. They can even learn to take food from a diver's hand. Taken captive, they live only for a short time and then die. Left in peace in the wild, they survive for 15 to 20 years. The female has a single pup every two or three years when food is abundant. Most of the otters' life is spent in the water, especially in places where many human beings live.

Once sea otters lived all along the Pacific Coast from Alaska to Baja California. Beginning in the 1700's, Russian fur hunters began killing the animals for their splendid pelts. So many otters were taken that they all but disappeared. A treaty signed in 1911 stopped the slaughter just in time. The otters in the Aleutian Islands of Alaska have become fairly abundant once more. Fur hunters are allowed to take a few animals each year. Alaskan sea otters have been transplanted to British Columbia, Washington, and Oregon, where small colonies are now beginning to grow.

The southern sea otter, native to California, is an endangered species. Although it has a refuge, it is persecuted by abalone hunters who do not understand that it is overfishing—not otters—that has caused the abalone to become rarer and rarer. If people insist on eating abalones, a way must be found to "farm" the shellfish, just as man farms oysters. Gathering wild abalones and shooting the otters can only bring about the eventual extinction of both groups of animals in California.

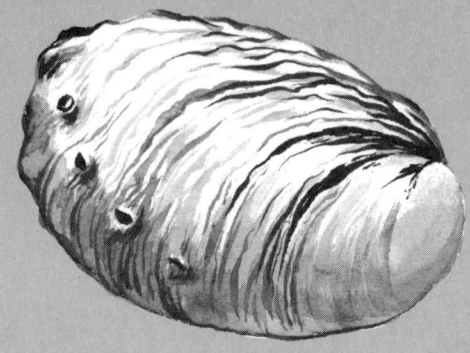

S. MAPLE ELEMENTARY SCHOOL